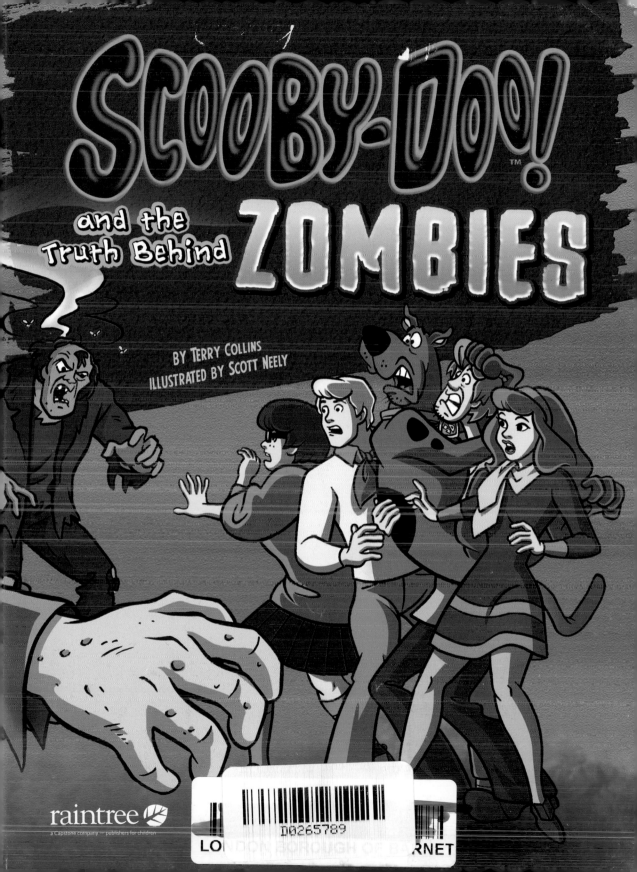

SCOOBY-DOO!
and the Truth Behind ZOMBIES

BY TERRY COLLINS
ILLUSTRATED BY SCOTT NEELY

raintree
a Capstone company — publishers for children

Raintree is an imprint of Capstone Global Library Limited, a company incorporated in England and Wales having its registered office at 7 Pilgrim Street, London, EC4V 6LB – Registered company number: 6695582

www.raintree.co.uk
myorders@raintree.co.uk

CAPG34574

Text © Capstone Global Library Limited 2015
The moral rights of the proprietor have been asserted.

Editorial Credits:
Editor: Shelly Lyons
Designer: Ted Williams
Art Director: Nathan Gassman
Production Specialist: Tori Abraham

ISBN 978-1-4062-8894-0 (paperback)
18 17 16 15 14
10 9 8 7 6 5 4 3 2 1

British Library Cataloguing in Publication Data
A full catalogue record for this book is available from the British Library.

Acknowledgements
We would like to thank the following for permission to reproduce photographs: Design Elements: Shutterstock: ailin1, AllAnd, hugolacasse, Studiojumpee

The illustrations in this book were created traditionally, with digital colouring.

We would like to thank Elizabeth Tucker Gould, Professor of English, Binghamton University for her invaluable help in the preparation of this book.

Every effort has been made to contact copyright holders of material reproduced in this book. Any omissions will be rectified in subsequent printings if notice is given to the publisher.

All the internet addresses (URLs) given in this book were valid at the time of going to press. However, due to the dynamic nature of the internet, some addresses may have changed, or sites may have changed or ceased to exist since publication. While the author and publisher regret any inconvenience this may cause readers, no responsibility for any such changes can be accepted by either the author or the publisher.

Printed and bound in China.

"Has anyone found Scooby yet?" Velma asked.

"The kitchen is all clear!" Shaggy replied.

"He wasn't in the Mystery Machine," said Fred.

"I've found him!" said Daphne.

"Scooby-Doo!" Velma scolded. "Why are you hiding in the sofa?"

"Rombies!" yelled Scooby.

"Zombies are nothing to fear," said Daphne. "You just need to know more about them."

Well, voodoo zombies are quite different from other legendary zombies. In voodoo, a *bokor*, or sorcerer, turns people into zombies.

A *bokor* gives his zombies a poisonous powder. The powder makes them his slaves.

"Are all zombies made by magic?" Shaggy asked.

"In films and stories, zombies are created in other ways too," Velma replied. "Chemicals and even zombie viruses can turn people into zombies."

"So, always cover your nose when you sneeze, Scoob," Shaggy joked.

Velma smiled. "No sneezing necessary. But a zombie's bite can infect you, and then you would become one of the walking dead!"

"Not that we're planning on looking..." Shaggy began.

"Uh-uh!" Scooby agreed, shaking his head.

"...but where can we find a zombie?" Shaggy finished.

"Wherever you want to look," said Fred. "According to legends, environment doesn't affect zombies. They can live anywhere."

"Zoinks! That makes it even harder to hide!" Shaggy said.

"If hiding is no good, can I outrun a zombie?" Shaggy asked hopefully.

"Yes, you can," Velma said. "Running away from a zombie is always the best response according to the zombie films. But remember, even though zombies are slow, they never get tired."

"Luckily, as their bodies decay, they fall apart," Fred added. "Zombies are often missing a foot or a leg. Even so, don't take them lightly."

Why? Are they stuck-up or something?
No, but often the only thing legendary zombies can say is "Uhhh, Uhhh." Their brains are mush, and some zombies have no tongues.
YUCK!

So, if some zombies have no tongues, what do they eat?
Scooby Snacks?
SCOOBY SNACKS

"Well, stories say that zombies eat fresh meat from any living creature," Daphne continued. "Birds, horses ... dogs."

"Ruh, roh!" Scooby exclaimed.

"And um, people," Fred finished. "Some zombies' favourite thing to eat is human brains."

Please don't feed the Zombies.

Why not? Ol' Frankie looks like a zombie to me!
Frankenstein was sewn together with body parts from lots of dead people, not just one. Also, the monster can think, he learns to talk and he doesn't want to eat your brain.

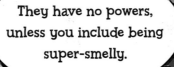

They have no powers, unless you include being super-smelly.

P-U!

A zombie smells of rotting flesh.

How can we protect ourselves against legendary zombies?
REAH!
Always carry something that makes a loud noise. Throw it away from you. Zombies will follow the sound, giving you a chance to escape.
RINGGG!

You should also always protect your body. Wear leather boots that cover your lower leg and feet.
Thick leather gloves keep hands and fingers safe. Layers of clothing help to avoid a zombie's bite. Also, never travel alone when zombies are about!

"Don't worry," Shaggy said. "With all of this great information, we can handle any old zombie that crosses our path! Right, Scoob?"

BRRRRAINS!

Move it, Scoob! Last one in the sofa is zombie stew!

"It looks like Shaggy and Scooby have found a great hiding place!" said Daphne. "Well, Scooby and Shaggy always were quick learners," laughed Velma.

GLOSSARY

chemical substance that creates a reaction

decay rot or go bad

flesh soft part of the bodies of animals and humans, made of muscle and fat

infect pass on a disease

legend old story handed down from the past

virus microscopic creature that can cause disease

BOOKS

Zombies and Forces and Motion (Monster Science), Mark Weakland (Raintree, 2012)

Zombies vs Mummies: Clash of the Living Dead (Monster Wars), Michael O'Hearn (Raintree, 2012)

WEBSITE

www.natgeotv.com/uk/zombies-the-truth
Learn about the origins of zombie myths and watch video clips, including a zombie survival guide.

INDEX